Soul Cookies

by

Janice Hoffman

HighTide
Publications, Inc.
Deltaville, Virginia

Published by High Tide Publications, Inc.
www.hightidepublications.com

Thank you for purchasing an authorized edition of *Soul Cookies*. High Tide's mission is to find, encourage, promote, and publish the work of authors. We are a small, woman-owned enterprise that is dedicated to the author over 50. When you buy an authorized copy, you help us to bring their work to you. When you honor copyright law by not reproducing or scanning any part (in any form) without our written permission, you enable us to support authors, publish their work, and bring it to you to enjoy. We thank you for supporting our authors.

Edited by Cindy L. Freeman
Book Design by Jeanne M. Johansen

ISBN: 978-1-945990-19-9

Publisher's Note: Some of the poems in this book first appeared and/or won various awards (in a few instances, under different titles or as earlier drafts) in literary journals and newspapers. The author has listed those titles and their respective publishing credits in the acknowledgement section beginning on page 104 of this book.

Dedicated with love to

Kenny, Jenny, Brian,

Daly, and Mama

Table of Contents

AWAKENINGS

Soul Cookies

Reading and writing poetry
has evolved into delicious

stolen moments to gasp in the luscious
breath of retrospect and revelation,

to capture minutes and to ponder.
Poems are little bits of bread

and sugar, nibblets of philosophy,
short and sweet like tea biscuits

in a London garden or perhaps
fresh baked goods from a warm

country oven. They bless and
delight, calm and entertain.

My mind is enlightened, my spirit
refreshed, so I scribble and savor

these delectable interludes and
devour these mini indulgences,

these idyllic little soul cookies.

MOTHERS AND COLORS

Eve

Because she longed to go deeper
into the woods of the Garden,
because she wanted to taste knowledge,
to hold its sweet juice on her tongue,
have it course through her blood,
and because he was still sleeping,
she arose early that morning.

Green cushioned her toes as she
took her time, knowing nothing of time,
and wandered past the mosses,
the clear waters, the bluebells
and irises that nodded and smiled.
She watched a squirrel open hickory nuts,
curious at how it persisted to the core,
how it understood ripeness.

Branches brushed her bare shoulders
as she approached the Tree. No briars,
no thistles held her back, prevented her
from the fruit, its form and fragrance
bidding her. As she sank her teeth into
the small, pungent globe, a current shot
through her, searing the bittersweet aftertaste.
Fire lit her mind, and the sun dulled
next to the blaze of her eyes.

Jochebed

Egyptian winds soften
as she treks from Goshen
to Raamses' palace,
answers the ad for surrogate.

Clandestine mother,
shadow nurse, she hums
to sleep the latest whim
of the princess.

She holds him,
whispers eternal secrets
to Pharaoh's newfound son,
plants immortal seeds

knowing they take root,
tap into ancestry, and
pledge deliverance fruit
sweeter than chains.

Vinnie's Villanelle

Emily Dickinson's sister Lavinia was her lifelong friend and confidante. They both embraced their mother's love of gardening.

Come outside to our sweet garden, My Dear,
and smell the lilac, sweet William, and rose.
No backyard is so vibrant as ours here.

Hollyhocks' dresses will allay your fear
and inspire both rich poetry and prose.
Come outside to our sweet garden, My Dear.

This morning I saw a lovely brown deer
nibbling till she spied me and then she froze.
No backyard is so vibrant as ours here.

What a wonderful, glorious green sphere!
Earth sings with this kaleidoscope of clothes!
Come outside to our sweet garden, My Dear.

Daisies and daffodils bring you great cheer.
Branches reach skyward; a gentle wind blows.
No backyard is so vibrant as ours here.

Here, sundry song birds surround us all year.
You can sing and write poems, I suppose.
Come outside to our sweet garden, My Dear.
No backyard is so vibrant as ours here.

Eastern Kentucky, Summer 1915

On a hill in Eastern Kentucky
sits an old woman in a cane chair,
two younger ones nearby, and
five barefoot kids on an elevated
edge of a dry creek bed lined with
smooth stones and dirt.

To the right, a black and white dog
smiles at the camera as if he waits
to herd the kids. On the other side
stands a huge elm with an empty
wooden chair leaning against it. A
sepia forest serves as a blurred backdrop.

A chicken stands on the threshold
of a rickety shack with no door.
Through the open doorway, it
scratches in and out as it pleases.
Cardboard covers the windows, the
planks of the shack worn and gray.

In this picture, my grandmother
is pregnant with the first of her seven
children, my great-grandmother and
great-aunt sitting before her, as patient
as the still, dry grass cascading
down the edge of the creek bank.

Sixteen years later, after a mass
exodus from Kentucky, my mother,
the sixth child, is born on a sultry
July afternoon, much like the one
in this picture. Eighteen and a half
years after that, she has me midwinter:

I'm born of the dirt, from salt of the
earth, strong women who endured
the Great Plague, crossing the Atlantic,
and summers in Appalachia—survivors,
like musty photos in old dresser drawers,
waiting to speak.

Mary Hester

paternal grandmother

Mary Hester never
leaves Kentucky.
Widowed twice, she
rears her seven orphans
on greasy green beans,
a razor strap, and
a worn, black Bible.

I take magic carpet
rides on her glossy
hardwood floors, and
I swing on her front
porch. I hear the train
whistle that always
blows a block away.

In my dreams, I tell
her the same chemotherapy
that failed her has also
failed my father-in-law.
She shakes her salt-and-
pepper head in pity but
doesn't even know she's
been dead sixteen years.

Hattie

maternal grandmother

My memories of her
are faint: soft, white skin
and watery blue eyes,
drab gray-brown hair and
a pale Orlon sweater.

She'd come to our 1950s
shotgun house and stay
just for lunch, then disappear
on the bus to Louisville
with a money order.

I loved her because she
was my mother's mother,
but I never really got to talk
to her except that time
Tommy and I went

to the hospital and
kissed her on the cheek.
She cried and we never
saw her again until the
funeral.

Cross Stitch

Acts 9:36-43

I heard him call my name:
"Tabitha," he said, and
I turned from my grey ancestors,
their arms bidding, waving toward
me to come to them, straw hair
and pallid flesh transparent.

"Tabitha," he said, and
widows I'd sewn coats and robes for,
the same women who washed
sweat from my body and laid me
in this upper chamber, hushed their groans,
looked up, startled at his authority,

powerful like a centurion, yet
gentle like our grandchildren.
He must have known,
known what words carry,
venom or honey, and how my ears
would drink his voice like medicine.

"Tabitha," he said, and
I crossed over and back,
like a stitch, understanding
the proverb: Death and life
are in the power of the tongue.
He spoke it once, and I opened

my eyes, saw him, and sat up.
Now I slip into my prayer closet
and, with breath born in my spirit,
weave garments of praise for
this man who spoke so sweetly,
the one who said, "Tabitha, arise."

Heritage

When I was a young girl with pale skin
and long, brunette braids, my mother told me
about a man named Remus Breeden who, one day,
leaned from his chestnut mare and handed

his Irish wife a bundle. She unfolded the
hand-woven blanket to find a copper-colored
infant. No one ever knew if Remus Breeden
found it, stole it, or if it were his own:

The baby was my mother's grandfather.

Part of me whoops war cries for my Anglo-Saxon,
Celt and German blood, and I dream eagle dreams:
I glide above knolls and knobs, silver maples
and white pines; I scan the Ohio River banks and

the rolling bluegrass of Kentucky. My flat cheeks
are like riverbed rocks, and my nose is straight
like an arrow. I'm tall and my bones are strong
like the oaks; my hands branch into long fingers.

During full moons, I sit in the yard with my dogs
and we remember wolf: we stare, recall eagles
and bundles, wigwams and sticks, tribes and packs;
we howl silently in cool darkness.

My white pride tries to suppress the primal
urge to worship, but I slip into storefronts,
speak with tongues of fire, spin and dance.
My blood pulses for the dirt of this land.

Colors of My Mother

My mother was born orange
and grew in the 1930s to bright
greens, the ones like the optimistic
and piercing wings of parrots.
Her teens were her ragtime of red,
flaming reds like the color
of her lips in that picture
where she's in a taffeta gown
in downtown Louisville,
at the Brown, I think, smiling
broadly, proudly, confidently.
After my birth and her divorce,
she turned darker, angry
as soot from an old stove,
but with my new dad and
baby brother, a yellow hue
shone from her again,
something akin to tangerine.

Years came and went,
the way years come and go,
and she began to embrace
tans, beiges, olive greens,
settled into the colors
of the mundane, the resigned.
But now, now, she is pastel—
lavender, lilac, pink,
soft greens like fresh
chartreuse buds in early May.

I talked to her on the phone
today, a new lilt in her voice,
newly encouraged,
newly revived as if she'd
received a transfusion of hope,
especially since this lymphoma
is slower than the cancers
that took both her breasts.
She's softer now, certainly
not ready to fade.

Red

She dreams of trees
and wolves, of forests
and wayward dogs.
In her dreams,
a man dressed in brown
with a sylvan scent
hears her gasp and
comes running. But
today, her scarlet cloak
covers her youthfulness
like an anointing
for dallying and picking
wild daisies and woodland
flowers. Her basket
overflows with sweet
breads and small cakes
as she nibbles and sings
along the familiar path.

When danger rears
its fanged, furry head,
her grandmother
uses the wisdom of age
like sage from her garden
and tames the beast.
In this version
of the story, by the time
the woodcutter springs
through the cottage door,

he finds the three—
the grandmother,
the girl, and the wolf—
sitting on a braided rug
rolling a ball and eating
fresh gingerbread cakes
before glowing embers
of a warm hearth.

Brown

The golden-haired
little girl crunches

through fall foliage
to a brown hut.

Uninvited, she
enters the door,

eats tan porridge,
sits on wooden chairs,

and drifts to sleep
atop a light chestnut

comforter. Startled,
she awakens to dark

eyes of three bruins
and runs home

through a dim forest,
craving color.

The Blue Fairy

She wears empathy like a holy cloak
over a gossamer gown the color of robins'
eggs. All the way to the verdant valley
and fruited glen beside the jagged creek,

she remembers the highlands and the sundry
gnarly trees, the mountain ash, the downy
birch, especially those beside brooks of cool
glimmering waters. She envisions golden

saucers of ambrosia and honeyed dew
sipped from teacups the color of cornflowers.
She recalls the pristine setting in her ancient
dreams. But tonight, she longs to help,

for in this new country with forests the color
of memory, she hears the midnight sobs
of an old woodcutter, leans near his open
window to see the waxing candles and

his wooden boy. Intercessor at her core,
she intervenes, raises her ethereal wand
like the scepter of a goddess, and grants the old
man's wish. An aura encircles her maternal

heart as the boy and the old man embrace,
thanksgiving cascading down the old man's
cheeks. She knows she'll return, but for now,
she floats away to her beloved homeland

of a thousand years, back to fields of hyacinth
and heather, back to clouds of blue hydrangea.

What to do with Old Pumpkins

I don't even get the word out,
just "Squu—!" and my dogs charge
down the deck steps into the backyard.

Onomatopoeia stirs them, delights me,
as dry leaves tattle on the squirrels
crunching about our grandson's

abandoned treehouse. They've discovered
the two leftover pumpkins we tossed out
to them and the occasional deer.

It's a Thanksgiving smorgasbord,
so they ignore our labs, frustrated and
running up and down inside a wooden

fence. I feel like a goddess on her lawn-
chaired throne, Juno atop Mt. Olympus
watching a golden panoramic view

of her domain. A crow caws through
the air; children call out in the distance.
Soft wind blows through the marmalade

treetops. Like the thorn bushes in Disney's
Sleeping Beauty, ivy and holly overtake
the treehouse. One squirrel sits on the tip

of her orange buffet, thankful for mortals
who live on the edge of the woods.

What Van Gogh Saw

an ekphrastic response to *The Starry Night*

During his time in Saint-Paul-de-Mausole,
light spilled across the heavens,
and everything was blue—
his glorious irises, his starry nights,
his self-portrait, his psyche.

The view from the iron bars of his window
included both the real and the remembered:
rolling hills on the horizon, dark green
cypress trees, the morning star that was truly
bright and visible that early dawn in 1889.

The village in his moonlit scene,
detectible only in daylight, was his Dutch
homeland, not Provençal—an imageaic
voyage of fantasy, not some type
of mental epilepsy the doctors feared.

"Hope is in the stars," he told Theo—
so he embraced swirls of ultramarine
and cobalt blue; citron, zinc, and Indian
yellow—Venus and her brilliant friends
beyond the asylum of his mind.

My Friend's Daughter

for Kaitlyn

My friend's daughter is blind,
but she hasn't always been,
so she remembers details
and shapes and forms and
rainbows of colors, of course.
Her favorite was purple.

She knew the medley
of beings: doors, desks, knobs,
teachers, and the preacher
till they all faded to pastels,
then grays and shadows,
then that cacophony of black.

In a crowd, she's invisible.
People forget that though
she can't see, she can still talk
and hear their muddled voices,
feel the distance in their stares:
She sees their gawking gapes.

She navigates her room
and taps through the hallways
in her assisted living home
on the arm of a nurse's aide.
She sings arias like a lark
that truly make people weep.

In the scheduled times of
darkness, when the unseen
moon declares night, she sleeps.
She dreams of plums and irises,
violets and deep velvet dresses,
struggling to rediscover purple.

Wrought Iron Skillet

Decades ago, a cold iron skillet
dominated Mama's kitchen.
It was heavy and black—the blackest
black a child could know.
On winter days, it cooked cornbread
in the oven: steaming, golden,
tender, moist. But best of all,
it baked cakes of plump cherries,
crunchy apple treats, and hot cobblers
with dumplings, berries thick
and gooey. Sundays after church,
it yielded chicken: lard crackling,
grease popping, pieces splatting.
Summer's catch fried in it:
blue gill and striped bass. Once
they swam in fresh, green lakes;
now they swam in that wrought iron
skillet, black handle gripped
by worn hands.

Sitting in a Doghouse

Here I am, nearly 39 years old, playing
with the kids and sitting in a doghouse.
I had to turn my mother-hips sideways even
to fit through the arched doorway. The fresh
straw on the floor has the same smell
my Easter chicks had in the 1950s. I scratch
the golden head of a confused Retriever
as I remember those worn, quilted tents
my brother and I would drape over kitchen
chairs and wooden clothes racks
near that black pot-bellied stove.
Hidden, we'd travel back in an invisible
time machine and become Roy Rogers
and Dale Evans, Marshal Dillon and
Miss Kitty, the Long Ranger and Tonto.
How were we to know of swollen bellies
in faraway places, a Cold War, and
the Bay of Pigs?

Frying Apples

Earlier tonight, I stirred apples frying in the
wrought iron skillet Daddy had given me;
I stepped back from the steam, the warm
scent of cinnamon, and thought about how
little margarine I'd used because it's gone up
to over three dollars a pound. Mama used to
send me to the corner grocer with 25 cents
in the late 50s and early 60s to buy real butter.
I wore pigtails then and can still see the cool,
white sticks in little brown bags. How many
single sticks of butter did I bring home back then?
how many nickel Cokes? how many chunks
of soup meat wrapped in white paper?

Red peels softened as I continued stirring.
Moments like tonight transport me to an
endless era where nothing ever changes: Mama
still bakes homemade pumpkin pies and banana
nut cakes with caramel icing; Daddy still stokes
the fire in the pot-bellied stove in our one-bedroom,
shotgun house; and Tommy still rides through
the side yard on a broom, screeching like the siren
of a fire engine. Even Sparky still tries to dig to
China, black dirt spread all over his spotted snout.
And somehow, the bad times no longer exist—
just those mundane, everyday moments, like digging
in the dirt and running next door for a stick of butter.

As September closes and we enter October,
I glory in the brilliant oranges and flaming reds
of the oaks and maples surrounding my home. Daddy's
gone now, and Mama lives in another state. But tonight,
when I dish up fresh, fried apples, I'll taste more than
fall fruit. I'll taste yesterday and hold it on my tongue
just a little longer than I should. Perhaps I won't talk
as much after dinner. Perhaps I'll skip the nightly
rituals, watching *Jeopardy* and *Modern Family*.
Perhaps I'll leave the skillet on the stove a while,
not wanting to wash away the scents of childhood.

First Born

Burst from my belly
violet eyes wide open
a gift from beyond.

Promise

for Jenny

The archetype of hope—
a child—

you are born
and shoot into my darkness
like a comet in winter.

Deep blue eyes
the color of continents of seas
—the iridescent ones.

Deliverer.
Baby messiah.

As you nurse at my breasts,
you breathe life
into me—

Over forty years later,
I still remember how

you held me
in your crystal gaze.

What Women Carry

They carry necessary things:
purses with pens and drivers' licenses,
old Kleenexes stuffed in pockets,
pacifiers and inhalers with meds,
recollections of hidden kisses.

They carry shame and guilt:
for acts they committed—
scattershot gossip—and those
acts they wish they had, unspoken
words too late to release.

They carry knowledge and alphabets:
BAs, LPNs, MBAs, MFAs, PhDs;
equations and poems fill their brains,
memorials to history and fallen
explorers and ancient philosophers.

They carry babies, genes, and DNA:
sons and daughters, stretchmarks,
loose skin and descendants
with blue or brown or black eyes;
memories and wishes.

They carry physical weight:
extra pounds after years of surgeries,
slowed metabolisms, poor choices—
chocolate instead of fresh fruit,
custard pies instead of veggie trays.

They carry psychological weight:
of those who have seen too many
of yesterday's ghosts, too many
of tomorrow's poltergeists, haunting
their minds, airing apparitions.

They carry nightmares, but also,
renewed dreams—and hopes—hopes
that their children will carry things,
too, that they'll carry the memory
of their mothers with them always.

Terminal Waiting

After answering a long-distance page
at the Indy airport, I wandered
from the terminal to a Target I'd seen
down the street. I continued my waiting
by allowing myself an unscheduled spree:
It cost me $16 and a penny,
but I came away with a plastic bag
filled with children's books
(though my children are grown)
and a paperback on my silent passage,
my biological clock, details of mood swings
and night sweats accompanying
the secret departure of my last eggs.

As I returned for the next arriving flight,
I entered the low-ceilinged parking garage
praying to God that I would live to witness
that final rite. I cursed cancer and tumors
that come merciless as Cossacks,
their bloody sabers wielding and hacking
wombs, breasts, and ovaries.
Like hideous hyenas, they eat away
at pale flesh and brittle bones and
turn daughters of Eve into bald men.
My fear of them has been consumed by rage,
those demons who slaughtered and devoured
my grandmothers and four aunts.

Reunions

In early morning dreams,
I remember the ones no longer here:

I glean wisdom like wheat
from grandmothers peeling peaches;

I make homemade buttermilk biscuits
with my aunts as we compare
the cadence in our middle-aged laughs;

the uncle whose parachute failed to open
grins as we drive to the annual family
picnic in his '59 Woody.

In this state,

I can redeem the time, hold it in my mouth
like a hot fudge sundae, smile and sigh

like I'm soaking in a powder-scented
bubble bath. Once again, my daughter's

barrette is tangled in her ponytail, and my son
comes home with rocks in his pockets.

I hold sleeping children
in aching mother-arms.

First You Weren't

for Daly

then, in a micro-moment,
two cells exploded
and you were a secret.
You germinated
raspberry, strawberry, rose –
embryo, fetus, child –
a pulp cradled in blood
and water, growing
to the flutter of the one
surrounding you

until that night
you fought dark liquids
and pushed toward
moonbeam,
toward your own
aurora borealis.
Will-o'-the-wisp,
you broke forward,
abandoned sanguine
fluids to gulp warm air.
You heard soft rivers
rush beneath your skin,

and now you dream
of berries and roses.

Old Fashioned Roses

Heavy under
morning rain,
my roses
drop their heads
and drink in,
each petal
glistening,
rehydrated,
refreshed.

This afternoon,
they'll turn
their faces
toward the
western sun
and grin
at a cloudless sky,
their fragrance
permeating
the side yard.

I'll stop,
sip the moment
and snap a picture
to remember
Mama—
and her roses,
slipped and
transplanted,
just like
her daughter,
thriving

Confessor

Isaiah 30:21

First born,
older sister,
head of the class,

mother,
teacher,
poet, preacher—

I now confess
that I need
a mentor,

an older woman
to take me
by the hand

and say,
This is the way,
walk ye in it.

Affinity with Blood

And what is this kinship we have
with blood? Some archetypal passion?
some pulse? some dream?

Primordials danced to its rhythm;
it poured from our mothers;
it's coursed through faceless caravans,
a red sea—something like water,
the core of an apple, liquid seed—
bonding a sacred, sanguine club:
great-grandmothers, daughters, strangers.

When my first child was being born,
my body thrust me into an ethereal
sorority, an uncharted realm;
I became a partner, inaugurated
into this ancient society where agony,
water, and cord blood are redefined.

Like night in November, this dark fluid
runs deep within us, and every moon,
a reminder. And even if silver scalpels
carve organs from our bellies, this blood
pulses in our brains, throbs in our chests,
and we love the gushing,

                       the living.

DARKER MOONS

Plantings

I once planted potatoes
in the dark of the moon,
quarters and halves
with eyes staring up.
To ward off bugs,
I sprinkled green powder,
the kind my mother and uncles
threw into flames during the '30s
to see sparks and light.
I scooped black soil
to build mounds, to hill them up.
The dirt kissed my fingertips,
sunk beneath my nails,
the sulfur at my nose.
Tonight, I dream I'm in that field:
My eyes turn upward,
my hands are black,
and I smell the soft green.
I feel the dirt, the pull,
the tapping into things
dark and deep.

Night Cravings

We camped by Lake Monroe where wharf rats
owned the picnic tables, the scant shore,
and we planned our futures teaching in Indiana.
Spring Mill. Deam Lake. Clifty Falls.
You performed the cherished cliché for me,
carving our initials in an old elm.

Tonight—twenty-six years later—
I curl my knees behind yours,
breathe your familiar skin,
and drink your exhaled air.
Our dogs dream at our feet, and
our children chase the night.

I am safe here—and for this moment
I dare to sigh, to pretend the planet
isn't spinning, that our autumn won't chill:
I pick bachelor buttons from forgotten fields,
watch a pocketknife claw brown bark,
wrestle with the dark.

Lunacy

The moon is always female. Marge Piercy

Full Moon, how dare you pull
the tides of her blood, jerk hormones,
then hide behind winter clouds!
She sees you bulging, peering,
acting innocent and bright. You
command devils to dance on her mind,
to chase her down the interstate where
your fiends pursue her like wild dogs.
If she tries to stop the insanity,
invisible quicksand swallows her whole.
Fat goddess, you are no sister spirit,
no sibling or comforting companion—
but a traitor, a witch who betrays,
manipulates, and casts spells.

Elizabeth I

From her throne
the Virgin Queen
peers out beyond
London's streets
and carriages

to make-believe
shores she'll never
dock, knolls
her royal slippers
will never touch,

forests her jealous
eyes will never
explore, so
she commissions
Raleighs and Drakes

as she grasps
her scepter, the
ball and chain of
her private Tower.

Queen Anne

reign 1702 - 1714

Twelve purple pulps
stained her royal sheets, then
one stillbirth and four dead
babies.

      Heir to her sister's throne,
she struggled not so much
with Marlborough as not to bleed
so much.

      Each lost prince,
each stolen princess,
seventeen times she died
a little more, but then one:

one boy, one son,
one miniature Duke of Gloucester,
a whisper of a king, pale yet
a living legacy

              toddling her empty palace.
Brunette ringlets framed
his small, round face and dark
moppet eyes set off his skin,

white like a snowdrop.
When he became ill, she watched
the Stuart line fade like scents
of lilacs in the air
             for a season.

Whispers from Elsinore

Yestermorning in eastern Denmark,
words travelled through thick, gray
walls like ancient osmosis, like water
through sieves from men inside to
wives outside and on to villagers
along dank pathways. They'd all
heard about fair Ophelia floating
and poor Yorick's skull, and even
about the Ghost. They knew about
apparitions, how they linger and
brood, some speaking, some haunting
to make a point, to obtain an end.
To what end was this visitation?
To let those in Elsinore's castle
discover what those outside already
knew? That murmurings matter?
That ambition is a beast so ravenous
it will devour its own?

When the mousetrap sprang,
the peasants already knew what rat
was caught in regicide. They heard
their young prince was beside himself,
that though Wittenberg had polished
his oratory skills, he muttered and
stumbled about the castle. What
they didn't know was how words
would convert to swords, how confusion
would reign more fervently than their

royals, how their prince would fall to the
feet of his friend, his final whisper,
O, I die, Horatio . . . tell my story.
Someone new would declare,
Speak loudly for him, and so it was,
even then, that what would remain
was what Hamlet spoke in the library:
words, words, words.

Offerings

"They believed their souls were in the blood." *Ancient Journeys*

Mayans and Aztecs fed on maize, beans,
and papaya; they worshiped the jaguar, snake,
and eagle and followed rulers like 16 Rabbit
and Montezuma in old Copán and Tenochtitlán.

Now steles tell victories with chiseled quetzal
feathers, faded turquoise, and hints of silver.
Did their captives, gifts to the Mezzo gods,
climb stoically up the stone steps to the altars,

heads held erect, proud and nimble as they made
the ascent to the bowls holding human hearts?
Or did they stumble, zombie-like, and reel
as frenzy and pageantry demanded their blood?

Polished obsidian sliced through living skin;
soldiers and priests carved out pumping muscles,
and gushes of blood forced souls into the wind:
The air still holds their silent howls.

Old Portrait at the DeWitt Gallery
Colonial Williamsburg, 2017

Portraits of Americana, patriarchs and matriarchs
cover the insured walls. Fathers and mothers and
children of the 1700s peer at guests visiting
these hushed rooms. In one, a mother holds her daughter,

ripe peach in hand, symbol of long life, three hundred
years ago. I stare and can see the breath of life
pulsing in their chests later, not now in this picture,
but as they hustle inside from the wind and snow,

cheeks flushed and pressed together while flames
in the open fireplace lick the room warm.
Mother and child embrace, breathe, wait for spring
and fresh grass, another day. The artist has painted

them eternal, like Shakespeare's beloved in Sonnet 18,
like Keats' couple on the Grecian urn, and here I am,
knowing they will outlive me, decade after decade,
three hundred more years. Suddenly, I crave a peach.

Battle

I don't believe in ghosts, yet twice—
once in Gettysburg and once in Yorktown—
a heavy breath of sorrow blew over me
unexpectedly.

I was simply tra-la-la-ing along visiting
historical sites as nonchalantly as a child
at play when interrupted. I felt the chill
of the marble monuments, heard the eerie

silence, the non-silence, the echoes of their
groaning. I didn't hear politics, no this side
versus that, but I saw ghostly uniforms,
vacant eyes grieving for another chance,

another lifetime, beyond blood-soaked dirt.
Here in the silence, I heard the price of war.

Foreshadowing Gatsby

a monotetha written for the Poetry Society of Indiana

F. Scott Fitzgerald had his dreams
and married Zelda as his queen.
They had plans, and they had schemes.
Or so it seems, or so it seems.

The Roaring Twenties made them soar,
brought prosperity to their door.
He worked and worked for so much more,
not to be poor, not to be poor.

They lived their lives in such great style;
they danced and drank and smoked a while
till so much excess caused them trials
and ceased their smiles, and ceased their smiles.

Flappers, fringes, the whole Jazz Age
put the two in a human cage.
She would cry and cause a rampage,
and he would rage, and he would rage.

Mary Ann's Sestina

Due to his mother's behavior following the deaths of her husband and three sons, Robert Todd Lincoln had her institutionalized at Bellevue Hospital. She was later declared sane and released.

In Lexington, many a rich and viridian boy
asks—begs!— me to come on down
and share a salad of dandelions, then run
to the strawberry fields with leaves of blue
and to the river's smooth edge to watch
the spring fish, rainbowed and so smart.

Madame Matelle tells my family I'm smart,
that my keen wit deserves as much as any boy's,
so they send me to finishing school to watch
my love of law and literature be gulped down,
to see my devotion to soirees and dresses blue
be nurtured, but sometimes I just want to run.

They say I'm a bit wild, that ladies don't run,
but I'm like a thoroughbred on our land, and smart,
so I move in with my sister; now I won't feel so blue.
Happily, here in Illinois I meet a tall man-boy
who loves me so and takes me on down
to buy nosegays; I buy him a gold pocket watch.

He courts me, doesn't care that people watch
the strolls, the carriage rides, the runs
through the town. I become his bride and down
the aisle I glide. In top hat and tails, he looks so smart.
Then come Robert, Eddie, Willie, Tad—our boys—
I'm happy as Kentucky's own sweet grass of blue.

I deliver fruit and flowers to our boys in blue,
support the Union with my husband and watch,
only to discover my own brothers enlist, Confederate boys.
The battles rage on and on like wild, angry runs
through nightmares. Our own plans are quite smart,
but then, like a twig house in a storm, it all crashes down.

Three of my children die; my beloved's cut down.
Why in the world do people ask why I'm so blue?
What good is it to be a socialite and so smart
if you have to survive and live on just to watch
all your dreams dissipate and savagely run?
My love's shot at the theater; disease kills my boys.

I thought I was smart, but life knocked me down;
then my last living boy made me even more blue.
They watch me in here; they know I will run.

Attachments

Each month when she sees clots
she thinks back to the IUD
the gynecologist said prevented pregnancy
when, in fact, she discovered
the only thing it prevented was wall attachments,
and she remembers that one particular clump
that seemed to have form.
Horrified, she panicked and flushed it
into the city cesspool, then tried to swim
an abyss to retrieve it.

She wanted to double-check, to see if
it had been her hysteria or if
there really had been a human tadpole
with head, arms, legs, central nervous system.
She longed to lullaby lost tissue,
sing songs of innocence to the color red,
and she wanted to know: how many?
how many of her clots had souls and
just how many swam away unsung?

Accidental Allegory

We'd stopped at a miniature
horse farm outside Gettysburg:

My husband, the dog lover,
discovered a newfound treasure;

our grandson, the adventure seeker,
became a small-scale cowboy;

I, the poet, dissected these small
equine creatures with new eyes

especially the tiny donkey
who was blind and moseyed along.

The day came to an abrupt halt
when a rabid possum staggered

near the wooden shack in back.
I grieved for the shaggy, gray

mammal, lost and reeling,
like the students in my classes,

some moseying,
some staggering,

all seeking salvation.

Cycles

Ekphrastic response to Samantha Gee's *Portrait of a Kitchen*

She stands at the sink
remembering
their first meal—
pork chops, peas,
mashed potatoes.

She watches the swirls
of water, cereal milk,
old brown broth
twist down the drain
year after year.

She stares at eddies
of goop churning and
curling into an abyss
after four kids and
one dead husband.

Tonight, she's alone,
drab browns and grays
no longer a sentence,
maybe a comfort
as her mind swirls,

empty and drained.

for Janie Chappell

c. 1893 - 1920

You lounge in a wicker chaise,
there in Kentucky in 1910,
and in this picture your eyes
pierce all the way to now, but
this is all before typhoid and
rheumatic heart. A wisp of air
through summer grass and elms
causes you to pause, put your hand
to your cheek; a gold locket rests
on your breast. Perhaps you're
thinking about morning sonatas
you fingered in the parlor or how
your hands strummed soft tunes
on a mandolin last evening.
Maybe you've just come from
picking day lilies and phlox near
the springhouse, from lattice work
and ferns. You sit there, seventeen
years old, in lace and white cotton,
like the peony at your waist,
fully bloomed and sweet smelling,
oblivious to petals falling,
to the fading of pinks.

Apple Tree

Daddy planted an apple tree
in our backyard when the kids
were little, and after a couple
years, it bore ripe green fruit.
Our two Golden Retrievers
would stand on their hind legs
and eat apples all summer
so that the tree was bare
halfway down but rich and
full on the top half. The kids
would help pick the ripest apples
in the fall, and we'd salt them
and eat them raw or bake them
in the oven with cinnamon
and sugar. When the kids got
older and we sold the house,
the new owners cut down the tree,
so the bees that came for its nectar
wouldn't sting their kids.
That one act stung all of us.

Mortality

Humanity's harlequin
stares back at her

from the mirror as
Death's hyena mask

cackles in her face.
The new doc

says her heart
beats at only 25%,

that she could drop
dead any moment

like a heavy rock
dropped from a bridge

just. like. that.

Daddy's Last Day

It's the eternal conflict of Al-Anon
adults, those grown kids of alcoholics,
the constant love-hate-fear struggle,
but as a child of the 50s, I knew of no
such groups or meetings, just the sting
of an angry hand or the rage and profanity
of one whose own mother tied him in a
basement for who knows what reason,
and then there was the time the Nazis
tried to cut off his Division at Anzio
Beachhead just like that clot that set up
a roadblock in his carotid artery and
the fierce explosion that raged in his
head one spring afternoon. He later
tried to tell us about the hairy bird on the
back steps whose real name was squirrel
and he picked wildflowers for Mama,
his only wife, her second husband because
her first one left her with me and no money,
but he arrived and bought me strained peas
and applesauce and gave me a baby brother.
His fingers bled in masonry and his lungs
filled with firefighter's smoke, yet
he taught me to ride that turquoise bike,
tie those black and white Oxfords, and
swim in the green waters of Lake Cumberland.
Faithful surrogate, he provided Cheerios,
hairspray, sausage pizza, college tuition,
and a wedding where he even played the

part of penguin dressed in a tux. Through
my life, he survived that stroke, cancer,
heart surgery, and diabetes, but on the
very last day, he gave me something
I don't remember ever receiving before:
a kiss on the cheek. Hours later, he shot
straight up in the hospital bed, threw up,
and died.

My Neighbor Doesn't Sing Anymore

At six, she trilled "Ring around the Rosie"
as she and her classmates all fell down.
In junior high, she swooned and sang
"I Wanna Hold Your Hand" with the
Beatles, and at high school graduation,
she hummed to "Pomp and Circumstance."
She wept during her wedding march, and
when her babies arrived, she lullabied
them till they grew and chanted their ABC's.

She moved next door to me about the time
she and her family joined the evangelical
church with guitars and drums. I'd hear praise
resonate through her open kitchen window,
and she always met me with a broad smile.
For the next two decades, her notes would
rise and fall with the cycles of living, but
the singing ceased the day two officers came
with news of her daughter's overdose.

Reckoning

for Brian

They say, "Write what you know."
I thought I used to know a few things:

how morning dew moistens the earth,
how Virginia cardinals swoop past my window,
how a baby's giggle makes me laugh out loud,

how my husband's eyes crinkle with his jokes,
how my daughter loves speaking Spanish,
how my son played the keyboard for me.

But now I know nothing.
I thought I knew how to pray.
I thought equations were fixed,

that 2 + 2 always equaled 4,
that 2 parents + 2 children =
a family of 4,
          but now

2 + 2 = 3 because 1 has
been subtracted, deducted,
taken away,
          self-murdered.

The math no longer makes sense.
Silent as his keyboard, I walk
through the years
          counting,

but it never adds up.

On the Anniversary of My Son's Suicide

"April is the cruellest month" from *The Waste Land* by T. S. Eliot

No, October is the cruelest month
where orange and gold pledges
are lies for what lies ahead,
where the darker solstice ushers
disillusionment and despair,
where Gaia and her satellite
spin souls out of sight.

I was sitting on a wooden table
in a forest when she gave me
a false preview of tomorrow,
of soft, cooler days and nights,
of autumnal flowers and flowing
leaves. She belied fairytales
which I too foolheartedly believed.

A red and black ladybug lit on the
thigh of my jeans, and I waxed poetic,
thought of calm breezes and tranquil
waters, of all that fall escorts in.
I looked up and around and saw a
palette of promises in the treetops
surrounding a friendly lake.

But not all Fujis and Galas crisp in fall's
orchards; bitter winds blow some,
faint and russet, to the unkind ground
to no ethereal rites of ripeness.

Eliot told the truth: "Dead trees give
no shelter." Solomon spoke reality:
"Vanity, vanity, all is vanity."

In a moment, with one sure shot,
October stole my only son—
so vibrant, so brilliant, so capable—
and my Adonis never returns.
But I return. Every October, my heart
converts to dull brown, and once again,
I dry and descend with the leaves.

Inductee

for Andrea

I don't dare tell my friends
I struggle with my faith—
except my closest one—
and I'm sure she prays
for my soul in secret.

But even my dearest
is not a member of our club,
the one we never wanted
to join, the one we were
ushered into wailing.

But you are. You joined
that rabid day your son
died, just like mine did—
yours from drugs,
mine from a bullet.

Do our ghost children
know each other? Do they
watch as we wretch
through the days, the weeks,
the months, the years?

These lines of abstractions
could not be more concrete,
more vivid, more hellacious,
more primal, more ancient,

more modern, more surreal.

Surviving mothers detest
this cruel conscription.

Cat and Mouse

We were touring the Wythe House
in Colonial Williamsburg when
through the thick boxed hedges

came a cat with a tail hanging from
its mouth like a loose shoestring
or a dangling spaghetti noodle.

A dog person, I'd never seen
the proverbial cat and mouse
game in person, so I stood still,

captivated as the scene unfolded
before me like a miniature play
in the Hennage Auditorium.

Kindly, or so I thought, the cat
released the mouse who, frozen,
lay there like a soft corpse, then

attempted its getaway. Like a
foosball player, the cat batted
the poor rodent back and forth,

then grabbed it once more
with its mouth, again and again,
small tail streaming from a feline

grin like a thin gray ribbon.
Today, as I muse over that lazy
summer morning, I'm thankful I've

escaped the years of your batting
me back and forth. My heart leaps
as it did that day the mouse bolted

from that cat, thankful not to play
your exhausting game anymore.

Echo

After your surgery, you whisper to me,
I don't think I'm going to make it, Sis,

    but I change the subject, insist
    that you fight—as if you might not.

I don't see you as a sixty-six-year-old
man, a retired FBI investigator

    with grown grandsons—but as the little
    blond-haired toddler bouncing

in the crib in the corner of our bedroom,
the three-year-old you racing down

    the sidewalk on your red tricycle,
    the younger brother playing with

painted turtles and guppies in the kitchen.
I see you waving an old bath towel

    in front of our dog as I hold him back.
    Toro! Toro! you shout, and I release him.

I see the sweaty twelve-year-old
hitting balls and running bases.

    Over six hundred miles apart, tonight
    you tell me over the phone,

You must accept the fact that I am dying.

I know it's true, but these scenes

      play over and over in my brain,
      and your words echo in my mind

again,
      again,
         again.

Sunset

I sit on our deck at dusk
and watch the evening sun
dip below the treetops.

I fear I'm at my sunset,
and like most, am not
ready for nightfall.

I am tired, but not of living.
I need to write, to pour
these decades onto pages

like watering a garden.
It doesn't matter if the
garden is small or large,

for it's the pouring
that's fulfilling, like
nursing my babies,

giving nourishment
to someone else. It's
the giving—and I'm

not empty yet, not yet
golden and not ready
to drop below the horizon.

AWAKENINGS

Rain

She sits at the metal table and chairs
thinking about rain. Cool and salt-less,
it softens what it touches:
                                She remembers
catching it in barrels for washing her hair,
mixing it with dirt to bake mud pies on summer
sidewalks, smoothing its drops over
her bare arms and legs.
                                Rain has memory:
it always returns to the air, then falls again
on fields, meadows, brick houses, concrete.
She stares out the kitchen window
to study its faithful vocabulary—
            drizzle,
                    sprinkle,
                                downpour
—then she steps out onto the deck
and into grass to wade through puddles.

The water washes over her toes, splatters
her ankles, and she's sure she's never felt
so clean—except when she was a child:

She'd run up and down the street's gutter,
splashing laughter into wet air, water streaming
down her face, her open palms, her young body,
and for all she knew,
                                eternity itself
consisted of those few saturated moments,
playing in rain.

Playing Marbles in the Dirt with My Brother

We were gods, you know, and
their destiny lay in our hands.

The orange ones were the cows;
the blue, horses grazing, all

corralled by dry twigs. A single
white one was a kitten dozing

on the porch and, of course,
the yellow ones, barnyard chickens.

Simple brown dirt was our Eden
as you and I laughed in the heavens.

Avian Moments

Leaves the color of tangerines
cling to branches as a black crow
waddles in the still-green October grass,
oblivious to my passing on a local road.

Snow blankets the fence on the edge
of my woods where a crimson cardinal
scatters and pecks, nibbling yesterday's
tortillas and leftover cornbread.

Like a sprite, a spring chickadee lands
on my worn, gray deck, and I swear
I almost see him smile. He tilts his masked
head and waits for me to join his chatter.

A green and purple hummingbird
hovers, then flits past my kitchen window,
a brief jolt of joy, serendipity on wings,
on her way to red petunias in a clay pot.

Lucia

Pale tourist on your white sand,
I sit waiting his return from bartering,
volleying pesos for t-shirts, baskets,
turquoise. You wander, barefooted,
to my towel, and our eyes meet:
yours so dark, shining like your Mexican
sun on this bay; mine, dull and gray
like my Midwestern suburb.

Up till now, I've refused
trying to talk to your people,
but I trust you, a child.
With my leftover high school Spanglish,
I discover you're about ten, just a bit
older than my daughter home
in Indiana with her grandmother
and little brother. I drop strange coins
into your small brown hand, and
you run to retrieve cokes for us.

You sit beside me, a delicate ambassador,
and stroke my hands. Your grin glistens
as I slip my diamond ring onto your finger;
brown and white intertwine like vines
on an abandoned gate back home.
We chatter and smile a while,
a microcosm of two neighboring nations.

When my husband returns,
I introduce you, my epiphany.
He waves his wares: a silver tray,
the Acapulco t-shirt, an Aztec blanket.
Lucia, that was seventeen years ago,
but my brain continues to carry you,
and sometimes—quiet, like today—
I take you out and look at you,
my sacred souvenir.

Calliope Dreams

The arresting voice of the steam organ
drifted up the hill to my shotgun house
like a dozen fireflies on a summer night.

I was about eight or ten, but that sound
captured me: the notes, light and whimsical;
the tone, a tender harshness.

Fifty years later and six hundred miles
away, I still hear the songs of the *Belle*
as the music floats up the river of my mind.

I'm carried away to another place,
another century. A young Sam Clemens-
like lad nods and waves me forward.

I stroll the deck of the paddle wheel
in my dress of mauve silk with a rose sash,
and I pass top-hatted gents in tails.

The water splashes the sides of the boat,
and twains are marked upon the river
as the keyboard sings on through my night.

Listening to Thunder

Sheets of rain pelt against the house
while distant thunder echoes for miles.
When I was a dreamy child,
I'd listen to the thuds of thunder
and remember Rip Van Winkle's tale
of magic and mystery in the Catskills
where the ghosts of Henry Hudson's
men ate cheese, drank wine, and
played nine-pins. Somewhere
along the way, I heard or added
Zeus and Apollo and other gods
bowling in the heavens. Occasional
crashes punctuate tonight's storm.
Trees bend, and boughs and limbs
crack and thwack to the ground
littering local paths and streets
like massive confetti. I've never
been to war, so no nightmares
haunt me during these mini tempests.
No, I'm comforted. I remember how
childhood thunder rattled the windows
of our old house. I relish the clashes,
the rumbling, the drum-like reverberations,
sorry when ceasefire calms the night.

Watchtowers near the Wetlands

Ring-billed gulls poke through
tourists' trash in the K-Mart
parking lot while their native
snow-white cousins sit atop
the river's pylons watching
for fish and clams in the James.

Blue and black herons stalk frogs
and insects near shallow marshes
from their nests in the treetops.
Because of their stunning white
plumage, the younger ones look
a lot like local snowy egrets.

A young horned owl sits on the limb
of a bare tree in the woodlands
near the edge of the water. He waits
for mice and squirrels, his huge face
and wide, sideways eyes piercing
the horizon as waves hit the shore.

A single, black crow hunts mussels
and worms from the apex of a green
wharf roof. His purple sheen will
dull tonight as he regroups with the
other members of his gregarious
family bantering and cawing.

A pair of bald eagles perches
on a massive platform of branches
near the water's banks, their white
heads and brown feathers signaling
their reign as they add even more
sticks to their thousand-pound nest.

Villanelle for Those Vernal Days

Embrace the time of robins and blue jays
For spring is the most divine time for love
Look! It's now winter, but along comes May

Now chase the gloom of darkness far away
Spread seed and crisp fruit for the turtle dove
Embrace the time of robins and blue jays

Erase the days of sadness and decay
Give thanks for plaintive calls of mourning doves
Look! It's now winter, but along comes May

Gather corn for cows; for horses, sweet hay
Hear the singing waters; smell fresh foxglove
Embrace the time of robins and blue jays

Come celebrate! Declare a new feast day!
Give thanks to all the heavens far above
Look! It's now winter, but along comes May

Let us now say good-bye to yesterday
Hurry along, and give Nature a shove
Embrace the time of robins and blue jays
Look! It's now winter, but along comes May.

The Christmas Tree

It
stood
a little
over six feet,
balsam branches
stretching toward
the ceiling, and you
and I were Buffalo Bill
and Annie Oakley. I still
remember you in that black
cowboy suit with even fringes
dancing from the sleeves, careful
not to back into the smoky Lionel
engine circling us. When I hit my
teens, I let you vanish in that smoke.
Now I'm glad I never saw you drunk or
heard you plead that night a pistol was
held to your head, and I thank God you never
saw Saigon. To this day, when I smell Scotch pine
on crisp December nights, I see colored
lights reflected in your eyes—and we're frozen
in 1956,
ever green.

Nature's Math

Under summer trees,
fireflies flit near a local
murky lake, and a dark
moon peeks through slight,
gray clouds hanging like
day-old laundry on backyard

lines. Stars peek through
fog. I consider the math
of the honeycomb I saw
earlier in the damp day.
I like the precision, the
geometry of the bees,

how meticulous and exact
they are in their buzzing
and humming and how they
fashion their craft, how
they fill each waxy receptor
with that syrupy colloid.

Weeks from now, back
in my home town, I will
awaken early and bake sheets
of generic cans of biscuits
and drizzle the sweet stuff
all over my plate.

Honeymoon

for Kenny

The Poconos had become
a cliché in 1970,
so you and I headed
from Indiana to New Jersey
in our VW bug.
Karen Carpenter crooned
that we'd only just begun
as we stopped over
in Pittsburgh and Philly,
city lights glaring,
nothing like the August
moon of the Midwest.

We landed softly
in a village outside
Atlantic City but made it
to the beach only once,
content with our plain room
in the local Holiday Inn,
the hamburger dive,
the white swans floating
on the placid lake with lily pads
and smooth stones—
those swans, that place,
the honeyed moon.

Diagnosis as Therapy

I guess they thought I was crazy
when I told them I heard music
during the MRI. Slipped into
a cylinder coffin, I lay there
and heard it: the *thump, thump*.
My brain throbbed with the beats
and threw together a chorus for back-up.
Thump, thump. No claustrophobia here,
but a few moments to sing
in my head the song of insanity
—or the songs of God.

Waves passed through me like light
through crystal. I felt their heavy notes,
each bass richer and thicker, filling me
with sound. I lay there and heard bullfrogs
on night ponds, grandfathers chanting 'round
campfires, Ancients dancing to earth rhythms.
I followed each note farther and farther
into myself. Blood and bones pressed together
—socket, sinew, vein—and I traveled time
and liquid, deeper till I reached the source,
till I merged with stone.

Kismet, April 2005

You and I strolled along
the brick sidewalks
one block parallel to
the Duke of Gloucester
in Colonial Williamsburg.
A soft breeze released
wisteria's perfume and
we were cloaked in hope
that spring. I was sure
I was dream-walking as
we glided through the day
on skates of air.

The afternoon sealed
itself when we entered
a college coffee shop
and Frank Sinatra crooned
overhead: "Fairytales
can come true; it can
happen to you – when
you're young at heart."
For that moment, peace
crowned us in its glory.
We reigned, briefly,
uninterrupted by tomorrow.

Visitation

When the first baby laughed for the first time,
his laugh broke into a million pieces, and they all
went skipping about. That was the beginning of fairies. J.M. Barrie

Orange-haired pixies
flit about and want me
to write a tale about them.
Lightning white starbursts
the size of day dust
flash around me from the
open blinds, and I wonder
that the other lung patients
in this waiting room
don't see sprites here.

It's a blessing and a curse
to see the unseen, to hear
colors and to smell textures.
But back to the fairies:
One wears a blue t-shirt
and leggings, her hair yellow
as a dandelion. Her friend
with the orange hair dons red
and covers her pixie lips
in surprise as our eyes meet.
The next one wears Cornish
blue with a pink tutu.

They dance in the ethereal
atmosphere around me,
these diminutive spirits of the air,
and I smell the aroma
of apples and gardenias,
foxglove and roses. I must

be at the edge of a Portal Tree,
somewhere between here
and the otherworld, maybe
in a contemporary fairy fort.

But it's midmorning, not twilight
or under the light of the moon.
I'm in a doctor's office, not
in enchanted woodlands of
mountain ashes or gardens
of herbs and rowan-trees.
Is it my British ancestry?
Am I a changeling?

Suddenly, I crave
berried jams and ales.
I hear a wooden flute
like a siren summoning me,
and I long to follow it.
It's Pixie Day in June,
and the hills are alive.
I finally know why I bought
tiny doll house furniture when
I didn't even own a doll house.

When other patients read magazines
and envision black and white
circles and squares, I see deep
rainbows of teal and yellow
paisley horses and dogs.
But then, in the flicker of a
moment, my fairies flee.
Shattered, I rise from my chair
as the receptionist calls my name.

Chocolate Lab Brothers

a triolet

My dogs chase their tails from morning to night,
and I laugh till I think I'm crazy.
You'd think they'd want to stop and fight—
My dogs chase their tails from morning to night.
They're such a silly, ridiculous sight,
but at least they're not dumb and lazy.
My dogs chase their tails from morning to night,
and I laugh till I think I'm crazy.

Dreamscape

Lost in Spanish moss and fog,
I stroll and breathe in moist air.

Deep green ivy and wild fuchsia
summer azaleas border soft grass.

Reaching arms of live oaks arch
overhead, high above the path,

and form a lush canopy.
The surroundings are surreal

yet as real as a waking dream.
This must be what the word

dreamscape looks like. I easily
imagine blue-haired fairies

with teal dresses and golden
lanterns floating through the air

and lighting on pink petals.
I want to linger here in the mist

of fantasy and wonder, in this
tender garden of soft what-ifs.

Concord, 2008

So much history in so few miles:
the little boy whose grandfather
heard the shot heard round the world;
the little girl who sat at his feet, not
knowing she'd write coming-of-age
novels to support her father who
considered himself a thinker;
the man who sold pencils and wrote
on borrowed land about a pond;
the temporary resident who penned
tales assaulting witch hunters.

I tour their homes, wade that pond,
visit their graves in Poets' Corner.
I've taught sundry students about
these three Transcendentalists and
their haunted friend—Emerson,
Alcott, Thoreau, and Hawthorne.
I've lectured on their thoughts and
theories, discussed their intermingled
ideas and friendships, but not until
I stand here in this still-sleepy village
do I comprehend the camaraderie,
the community of unsolicited harmony
they shared within these few miles.

I ponder this: that a few drew together,
that some men and a woman wrote,
that they reasoned and deliberated

and released their words into history,
sound waves into the universe—
for me, for my students, for myriad
more, for thinkers and dreamers and
millennials, for those who would read
and think and contemplate beyond
the moment, beyond cell phones
and selfies, beyond themselves.

An Adjunct at School

The young rush
from class to class,
but I'm old now,
so I stop suddenly
because I smell
something.
          The air
is thick and sweet.
I look around—
no blooms,
no flowering shrubs.

I look down—
the ground is carpeted
with uncountable
clover,
        fat and white
in green grass.

I breathe deeply,
an old woman
on a college campus
taking sensory notes
for her students
as they brisk by

unaware.

Now that I'm Old

I once was young and thin and tall
This was before cataracts, after all.
But now I'm short and fat and old
with several fake parts, if truth be told.

A defibrillator controls my heart;
my CPAP helps my lungs restart.
I also find it quite ironic
that titanium hips now make me bionic.

But if there's hope somewhere to be found,
it's that I'm still on top of the ground!

Blue Ridge Worship

Fresh green branches pushed aside reveal a small
opening with a clear spring running through it.

The sun shines down, and its rays make the shoals
of the shallow stream shimmer. Along its banks

is clover, the kind small rabbits nibble. Soft grass
carpets the floor of this hidden setting

as low-hanging branches canopy a secret. Sometimes,
this secret is lush and yellow-green, and scents

of honeysuckle hang in the air. Later in the year,
the little stream freezes over just on the top so that

the water rushes beneath its surface. Often, hoof
and paw prints from wandering deer, fox, and raccoon

interrupt the snow. When warm air returns, wild
violets splash over the ground, blackberries burst

from bushes, and squirrels scamper about and pose
like little brown teapots. Amidst this holy shelter,

all living things tap into tranquility. I attend this
primordial church at dawn when soft hills whisper

daybreak, as sun and moon slide into each other
melding orange and pink across a cobalt sky.

Poet's Prayer

[A dreamer] can only find his way by moonlight,
and his punishment is that he sees the dawn
before the rest of the world.   Oscar Wilde

Let me dream of oranges and rats tonight,
something like the psychedelic tigers that
danced in my bedroom after the last D & C.

Let me dream in Technicolor one more time,
to peel the eyelids off sleepers and to stir
the silent fountains of my friends.

Let me dream of red revolutions
and perennial flags of green and blue,
celestial infernos burning the sky,

And I swear, when I come out from
under the patched comforter of Morpheus,
when I awake from electric paint,

I will dig for you verbs to pluck passion,
adjectives and nouns to root out fiends,
and prophecies to caress your own faint heart.

musica humana

> *From harmony...this universal frame began.* John Dryden (1687)

Creatures of music,
our lives are orchestrated
between lullabies and dirges.

Chant, warble, yodel,
we're driven toward harmony,
toward meter and chords.

As children, we giggle piccolo
moments in violin dramas, then grow
to the beats of praise, rage, melody.

Our brains throb like kettle drums,
and we live and love
pianissimo, crescendo, rest.

From waltz to worship,
ragtime to rap,
we celebrate movement;

from labor contractions
to death rattles, we crave rhythm.
And after we die, we twirl

into eternity past stellar bodies,
pirouetting through galaxies,
ever singing.

Right before Falling Asleep

Weave a tale of hollyhocks
Braid a chain of clover
Awaken all the four-o'clocks
Stop before it's over

Flowers tumbling through my head
Words born of fairytales
Dreams and visions amply fed
Take wing and set to sails

If I die before I wake
Put my poems in pages
Give me lots of chocolate cake
Make me live through ages

Acknowledgments

I wish to express my heartfelt appreciation to the following literary journals and newspapers in which some of these poems first appeared and/or won various awards (in a few instances, under different titles or as earlier drafts).

"Soul Cookies"	Poetry Society of Indiana
"Avian Moments"	*Snowy Egret*
"Elizabeth I"	*Kentuckiana Metroversity;* Poetry Society of Virginia
"Eve"	*Tantra Press*
"for Janie Chappelle"	*Women Who Write*
"Frying Apples"	*Hausers*
"Hattie"	*IUS Review*
"Heritage"	*IUS Review*
"Jochebed"	*Daughters of Sarah*
"Lucia"	*POEM*
"Mary Hester"	*IUS Review*
"The Christmas Tree"	*IUS Review*
"*musica humana*"	*Canadian Writers Journal*
"Night Cravings"	Poetry Society of Indiana
"Plantings"	*Plainsongs*
"Poet's Prayer"	*POEM*
"Rain"	*Snowy Egret*
"Reckoning"	*The Daily Press*
"Sitting in a Doghouse"	*The Windless Orchard*
"Villanelle for Those Vernal Days"	Poetry Society of Indiana
"Watchtowers near the Wetlands"	*The Avocet*
"Accidental Allegory"	*Pegasus* (Kentucky State Poetry Society*)*

"Foreshadowing Gatsby"	Poetry Society of Indiana; *PSI Anthology: Ink to Paper*
"Diagnosis as Therapy"	*The Northern Virginia Review;* Poetry Society of Virginia
"On the Anniversary of My Son's Suicide"	South Dakota State Poetry Society; *Pasque Petals*
"Lunacy"	Illinois State Poetry Society
"Playing Marbles in the Dirt with My Brother"	Poetry Society of Texas
"Colors of My Mother"	Oregon Poetry Association; *Verseweavers*
"Mary Ann's Sestina"	Poetry Society of Virginia

I also would like to thank Sena Naslund for her instruction and Sharon Dorsey and Linda Partee for looking over my manuscript and giving helpful feedback. Many thanks to wonderful friends and family—especially my husband Ken, daughter Jenny, son Brian, grandson Daly, and mother Peggy—who have been so patient and encouraging over the years. Finally, thank you to Jeanne Johansen and Cindy Freeman at High Tide Publications for their guidance and for making a dream come true.

About the Author

JANICE HOFFMAN holds bachelor's and master's degrees from Indiana University and has taught creative writing, expository writing, and literature in Indiana and Kentucky. Currently, she teaches at the Historic Triangle Campus of Thomas Nelson Community College in Virginia where she also co-hosts a monthly poetry reading.

She is a member of several local writing groups, as well as the Poetry Society of Virginia for whom she edits *A Commonwealth of Poetry*, its newsletter. She is also a member of the Chesapeake Bay Writers and the Poetry Society of Indiana.

Her work appears in sundry literary journals (*Snowy Egret, POEM, The Northern Virginia Review, Women Who Write*, and others) and has won awards and/or also appears in the anthologies for the poetry societies of Indiana, Kentucky, Illinois, Texas, South Dakota, Oregon, and Virginia. In 1995, she won first place in *The Canadian Writers' Journal's* international poetry contest, and in 2017, she was runner-up for Poet Laureate of Hampton Roads. She lives in Williamsburg, Virginia, with her husband, grandson, and two Chocolate Labs.

She can be reached at janhoffpoetry@gmail.com, on Facebook at janhoffpoetry, and at https://sites.google.com/view/janicehoffmanpoetry/home. Her book is available via Amazon.com, Barnesandnoble.com, and IndieBound.org.

www.ingramcontent.com/pod-product-compliance
Lightning Source LLC
LaVergne TN
LVHW091310080426
835510LV00007B/457